A   P   O   C   K   E   T   B   O   O   K   O   F

MARBLES

AN OUTLINE PRESS BOOK

© William Bavin 1991
First published in Great Britain in 1991 by
Outline Press (Book Publishers) Limited
115J Cleveland Street
London W1P 5PN

This book was designed and produced by
OUTLINE PRESS

Design: Sally Stockwell
Photography: Garth Blore

The author wishes to thank
Mr Sam McCarthy
of The British Marble Board of Control

CONTENTS

THE HISTORY OF MARBLES

 No one really knows when the game of marbles started, or when the first marble was made. It is probably fair to say that, in one form or another, they have been around almost as long as mankind.

Archaeologists have found game boards and playing pieces in the earliest excavated graves in Egypt and the Middle East and in most other parts of the world. Little white marbles and round pebbles were found in Austria in caves inhabited by our paleolithic ancestors. They were not made of local stone so had obviously been imported. One can only speculate about their use, but they must have been of some value to their owners to have been kept and carried with them. Stone balls and pillars to form an arch were found in a child's grave in Egypt which was dated at around 4000 BC.

The early Greeks played various games with nuts. One of these, called Omilla, was very similar to the game of Ring Taw which is still played today. There are frequent references to marbles and marble type games played with nuts throughout Roman literature. Ovid describes various nut games in his poem 'The Walnut Tree'. It is probably fair to assume the Romans took this popular form of entertainment with them to all parts of their empire. Children playing marbles appear in Roman murals in Bath in England. Clay marbles have been found in a settlement influenced by Roman culture in North Western India dating from the second century AD.

We know that 'marbles' was played throughout Europe. There are mentions of the game in Shakespeare. The Czech educationalist Johan Comenski talks of them in his book of 1658 and they are seen in a painting by Pieter Bruegel.

The earliest marbles were made of common stone, in some cases real marble, and clay. Coloured glass marbles are mentioned as early as the fifteenth century in German literature and were known to have been made in Venice and Bohemia at this time. It is assumed that these early glass marbles were not made commercially, but were made by glass workers for their own children at the end of the day.

China and crockery marbles were introduced around 1800 and were produced in increasingly large quantities until the end of the century. By the middle of the last century German glass blowers had invented a tool to cut marble canes more easily. These specially adapted shears meant that production became quick enough to make the sale of glass marbles for the public an economic proposition. These marbles became increasingly popular throughout Europe and America. An enormous variety of colours was used and intricate patterns were created within the glass. Stone, agate and marble marbles continued to be produced, mainly in Germany in special ball mills, and clay marbles began to be produced in bulk from about 1870 onwards on both sides of the Atlantic. In the 1890s, the first machines for the manufacture of glass marbles were introduced. However, machine production remained low until the First World War in Europe cut off supplies of marbles to North America. This stimulated the production of machine-made marbles in the USA, to the detriment of European glass and stone marbles. This production technique and the machines themselves are now found in many countries east and west.

● *'Marbles' from 'Juvenile Games for the Seasons', 1823.*

These days, marbles are made from all sorts of materials, but glass remains by far the most popular. Glass lends itself to both hand and machine production and provides an article which is both appealing to the eye and to the touch. The rather boring clay and compressed stone marbles are hardly made at all now and the beautiful ground agates and real marbles have become so expensive that only one or two mills in Europe and India still make them.

A marble made of pure, ground marble, or other suitable stone, is highly prized and regarded as being the most accurate for shooting, but the most beautiful marbles and the most sought-after by the collector are the best of the glass marbles.

MAKING MARBLES

MARBLE, AGATE AND OTHER STONE

These are the traditional marbles, still produced in Germany and parts of India. The rock to be made into marbles is cut into small cubes. The cubes are placed in the grooves of a marble mill. Each mill consists of a heavy and fixed horizontal mill stone with up to twelve concentric grooves cut into it. Iron balls of the marble size required are also put in the grooves. Above this mill stone is a large, round slab of oak or beech the same size as the lower block. The whole apparatus is positioned where water can turn this upper slab. As the wood turns the rock cubes are ground round to the size of the iron balls. They are then removed from the mill and finished in a polishing barrel.

MAN-MADE STONE MARBLES

To our knowledge there is only one factory left making these; it is in southern Sweden. This marble-making technique uses a machine which resembles a cement mixer. The machine is filled with a slurry comprising plaster, cement, talc and pigment. Tiny rape seeds are thrown into the mixer and roll around inside. As they become moist they begin to pick up a coating of the mixture, gradually increasing in size and becoming round. Several hours later during the process coloured dyes are added to give the marbles their required colour.

● *Semi-precious Tiger eye.*   ● *Delicate and beautiful Rose quartz.*   ● *Unusual Labrador Bay rock.*

● *Semi precious stone marbles — beautiful and prized as the most accurate to shoot.*

CLAY AND CHINA MARBLES

Clay and china marbles were made in similar ways. There were various techniques, but, to generalise, the mass of clay or porcelain would be forced through a pipe to form long cylinders which were then cut into equal-sized pieces. These pieces would be pressed or rolled into spheres using wooden drums/rollers. They would then be dyed or painted with patterns and colours and placed in a kiln to be fired.

STEELIES

The vast majority of steel balls, of course, are made for industrial use. However, various sizes of steel balls form an important part of most childrens' marble collections. Steel wire is cut into equal-sized pieces and each piece is pressed between hemispherical dies into a ball shape. The balls are then machined in filing mills similar to those described for making stone marbles. They have one fixed and one rotating plate but unlike the stone marble mills there are concentric grooves in both the plates, which are made of cast iron.

HAND-MADE GLASS MARBLES

There are many types of hand-made marbles and these will be covered in detail in the chapter on collecting. The basic method of production is the age-old glass makers' technique. A glob of clear, molten glass is gathered on the end of an iron rod. Colour is added either in the form of pre-prepared, coloured glass canes or in the form of chips of powdered or granulated coloured glass, depending

The glassblower rolls the coloured glass on his 'bit iron' into a long cylindrical 'cane'. Using special tools he forms a marble and shears it off. Several marbles are made from each cane.

on the desired effect. A large glass cane is built up to the pattern and colour desired and of a width the size that the marble is going to be.

The glass maker sits in his chair rolling his iron on the arms backwards and forwards (as illustrated on previous page). The end of the cane is reheated in a small furnace called a glory hole. When the glass is pliable enough to mould, a shear is used to cut off the right amount of glass to be formed into a marble. The glass maker rounds the end of the cane carefully as he rounds off the point at which he is cutting. As the glass is continuously revolving with the movement of the iron, the marble becomes completely spherical and is eventually severed. It is then put into an annealing oven to cool down. Several marbles are made from each of these large canes.

Thin, coloured, glass canes are used for making elaborate spirals and swirls, glass grits are used for making 'end of day' or spotteds, mica and copper filings are used to make snow flakes and other patterns.

Small, pre-prepared clay figures are used to make the most prized marble of all which is the sulphide. These clay figures are inserted into lumps of clear glass which are then formed into marbles. These marbles are made individually.

———————— MACHINE-MADE GLASS MARBLES ————————

The actual manufacturing process appears quite easy, but technically it is difficult. The glass is melted in a large furnace and when it is at the right consistency it pours out through an opening. Shears set at the opening cut the descending glass into equal-sized pieces. These pieces drop into moving, mechanical rollers which have spiralling grooves running down their length.

The globs of glass travel down these grooves, gradually cooling and forming into the round marbles. When they reach the end they drop into metal containers where they collect for annealing.

For clear marbles the batch glass is melted to the colour required. For leaf and cat eye marbles with different coloured inserts, a fore-hearth is used at the front of the furnace to inject different coloured glasses into the main body of flowing glass prior to it meeting the shears. For rainbows, oilies, spotties, etc., various chemicals and chips of glass are applied to the outside of the hot marble when it is almost formed.

● *A selection of machine-made marbles and coloured glass in 'cullet', cane and powdered form.*

COLLECTING

 Marble collecting is taken very seriously by adults who have become addicted to antique marbles. In the USA in particular there are thousands of collectors. Rare antique marbles change hands for hundreds of dollars and for several thousand dollars in the recent case of a sulphide featuring a bust of George Washington.

No less addictive, however, is the collecting of more modern, machine-made marbles. This is something practised by children in

● *Antique and modern, spirals and swirls — showing the glassmaker's skill at its best.*

most parts of the world. These collections are generally built up by swapping and by winning them at play. As with antique marbles, the most beautiful and rarest examples are the most sought-after. Companies like House of Marbles in England continuously produce new and interesting designs by machine. There are now hundreds of different types from their range alone to be collected. Amongst these, the collector must always be on the look out for the 'one off' interesting mistake which leads to something unique, i.e. an interesting pattern of bubbles or a lump of furnace brick trapped in the glass.

Another range for collectors is the modern hand-made marble. There are several glass studios in the USA and the House of Marbles in Devon, England, which now make works of art in the form of marbles as manufacturers have done with paperweights for many years. Elaborate and beautiful designs are produced in the round. These marbles are expensive, but are highly valued by those who appreciate the beauty and skill involved in their making. Modern, hand-made glass marbles come in all sizes and are generally in mint or near mint condition. The variety of designs is enormous and because they are regarded as works of art they are difficult to categorise.

There is no point in giving a price guide here, as prices change from year to year. However, the Marble Collectors Society of Trumbull, Connecticut, USA, publish a price guide periodically. To our knowledge, there is no equivalent publication elsewhere in the world so a collector must be sure to buy only after making price comparisons in the marketplace.

Mainly nineteenth century · Sizes – generally from 12.5mm-60mm (½in-3in). Condition – Mint, near mint, good collectable.

Swirls Transparent glass with stripes of colour often around a centre core. There are solid cores, open cores, cores of latticework and an enormous variety of colours.

Lutz As the swirls mentioned above but with stripes of copper filings which make them sparkle. Named after a New England glass maker but many thought to have been made in Germany.

Clambroth Striped swirls on creamy background. Mainly produced in the USA at the turn of the century.

Indian and Peppermint Swirls Opaque marbles of various colours and black with bright stripes on the outside. Origin not known but probably the same as Clambroth.

Micas Snowflakes Transparent marbles with chips of mica added. Found in all the basic colours but ruby reds are very rare.

End of Day Made individually, they only have a pontil mark at one end which shows they have not been cut from a rod. They are thought to have been made at the end of the day by glass makers using up left-over bits of glass to make marbles for their children. They can be extremely old and scarce. (Pontil, pronounced 'punty' is a glass blower's iron.)

Onionskins Grains of coloured glass are gathered on a gob of clear glass and then another layer of clear glass is gathered over this. A multi-coloured mottled effect is achieved. Mainly European in origin.

Opaques Rather uninteresting marbles, but always popular for some reason. Known as slags when the surface is randomly striped white on a dark background.

Clears Like opaques, clearies have always been popular. They show how many beautiful colours were available to the glassmaker.

Sulphides The most prized marbles. A clear marble with a clay figure in the centre, mainly of famous people, animals, trains, etc. Mainly German, second half of the nineteenth century. Coloured sulphides are very rare.

Agate and Stone Produced mainly in Saxony during the eighteenth and nineteenth centuries but still being made today. Popular because of the infinite variety of colours and stripes of the stones.

Gemstones Mainly European, like agates and other stone marbles – but made of semi-precious stones from all over the world – tiger's eye, malachite, quartz etc.

China Again, mainly European from the last century. Huge variety of glazed and unglazed, linear patterns and floral decorations.

Clay and Crockery These two categories are amongst the least interesting visually and are quite common. So, although in some instances they are very old, they are not so highly prized.

Comic Strip Marbles Produced by Pelltier Glass Co. of Illinois they were only produced for a short time and are scarce and desirable. Popular comic figures are depicted on each marble.

● *Antique marbles from the author's collection*

——— MODERN MACHINE-MADE MARBLES ———

Sizes from 12.5mm-35mm ($^1/_2$in-1$^1/_2$in). Condition categories same as antiques. There are thousands of different names given to each type of machine-made marble so we are only going to describe the general categories.

Clears Almost every colour you can imagine is now available as a clear glass marble.

Inserts, Leaf The most popularly produced marble for fifty years from the 1920s to the 1970s. An individual pot of coloured glass is used to inject a leaf of colour into a mass of clear glass. The leaf can have several canes and can be of a single colour or of mixed colours.

Inserts, Spaghetti, Cat Eyes Same process as described with leaf, but the effect is a random scattering of twisted canes within the glass.

Glass Chinas Opaque glass with stripes of colour on the surface. A huge variety of different coloured stripes have been used over the years on different backgrounds. This type were amongst the earliest machine marbles produced. Manufacturers often tried to reproduce the look of natural agate.

Opaques A completely plain opaque colour, now produced like the clears in a large number of colours.

Spotted (opaque or clear) Chips of coloured glass are rolled into the surface of the marble before it is cooled.

Frosted (opaque or clear) A finished marble is treated in an acid bath. The process can make an uninteresting marble great.

Lustered (opaque or clear) The application of chemicals by spray to the skin of a marble as it is being made produces this iridescent effect. They are known as rainbows, oilies, pearls or lustres.

——————— OTHERS ———————

Steelies Come in many sizes and qualities. Cheap ones rust.

Magnetics Plastic with a magnet inside. Unattractive but fun.

Brass Very rare.

Stone Still being made but expensive.

Clay, Man-made Stone Production very limited now as they are not very attractive.

Modern, printed marbles Pad printers are used to print characters or advertising logo on the outside of the marble. This print will rub off if the marble is used regularly in play.

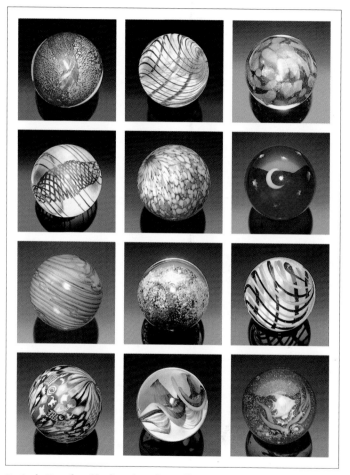

● *A selection of marbles from the author's collection.*

PLAYING WITH MARBLES

---------- *SHOOTING* ----------

The most common method of shooting a marble along the ground is known as 'Fulking'. The knuckle of the forefinger is put on the ground and the marble is balanced in the bent forefinger. The thumb is put behind the forefinger and then released with whatever force is required.

This method, however, is less accurate than 'Knuckling Down', which is the method used by experts. The marble is held above the first joint of the thumb by the tip of the forefinger. The top of the thumb is held by the middle finger. The hand is kept quite still with the knuckles on the ground. The thumb is released with the required force. With practice great accuracy may soon be obtained with this method. In India they have an altogether different method. The thumb and little finger are placed on the ground and

● *'Fulking.'*   ● *'Indian' method.*

the marble is held against the middle finger which is pulled back, like a catapult, and released.

Marble games are generally played with cheaper glass marbles, but when expensive and special marbles are used in games, where fines are imposed or where marbles are lost or won, it should be agreed in advance that fines or losses should be paid in cheap marbles and not with the player's expensive and prized Shooter or Allies.

Names given to marbles vary considerably from town to town within each country. The best marbles are often known as 'Allies'. A marble actually being used by a player is often called a 'Taw' or 'Shooter' or 'Tolley'. We shall use the word 'Taw' when explaining the following games.

When aiming, it should be remembered that the target should be steadily looked at, its exact position being thoroughly taken in by the eye while the marble is held in the hand. The eye directs the brain which automatically directs the hand.

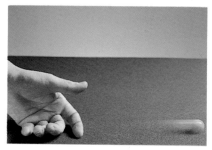

● *'Knuckling Down'* — *for accuracy and speed.*

● *'Archboard'* — *to score the most you must risk the most.*

——————— *ARCHBOARD (OR BRIDGEBOARD)* ———————

 For this game a piece of board is required with seven or nine arches cut in it. The central arch is numbered '0', the arches on either side of the centre are valued '1'. The values increase the further the arch is from the centre, i.e. 3 2 1 0 1 2 3.

One player is made bridgekeeper, the others shoot marbles at the arches from a distance of 1.5m (4 to 5ft). Those marbles that fail to pass through an arch are taken by the bridgekeeper. For every successful shot that goes through an arch, the bridgekeeper must pay the shooter the corresponding number of marbles to the number shown above the arch and those marbles should be the same size as the marble shot through the arch. A marble passing through the centre arch marked 0 is returned to the shooter with no reward. Every player should take his turn at keeping the bridge.

BOUNCE ABOUT

This game, for two to four players, is played by throwing marbles and not shooting them. Medium-sized marbles are best suited for the game and are called 'Bouncers'.
The first player throws his Bouncer forward 1.5m (5ft). The second player throws his to try and hit it. The third player throws to try to hit either one on the ground and so on. If a Bouncer is hit the owner must pay the successful thrower one marble. Bouncers are generally not forfeited.

BOUNCE EYE

A circle 30cm (1ft) in diameter is marked on the ground. Each player puts one marble in a pool in the centre of the circle. The players take it in turns to stand over the circle and drop a marble from eye level into the pool of marbles. Any marbles knocked out of the ring become the property of the player. If a player fails to capture any marbles with a drop, the marble he has dropped remains in the pool. The game continues until the pool is dry.

This game is similar to Bounce About but the marbles are shot and any size of marbles may be used by any number of players. An order of play is decided. The first player throws forward a marble to whatever distance he chooses. He will generally choose the distance at which he personally shoots with the greatest accuracy.

The next player then shoots at this marble. If he hits it he captures it and it becomes his property. He then throws out a new marble to restart the game. If he misses it however, this marble remains in the field. The third player then shoots at either marble,

● *You keep all the marbles you hit in each turn.*

capturing whatever he hits, but leaving his marble in the field if he misses. If a marble is shot with force and bounces off several marbles in the field, then all those hit are captured.

In this game there are no niceties. If a player shoots with a rare and expensive Taw he may have the advantage of accuracy over the other players, but stands to lose his Taw to another player should he ever miss.

● *With a good shot and lots of luck you can win six marbles in one turn.*

DIE SHOT

 A die is balanced on a marble which has been ground down slightly for stability. As in Archboard, players take it in turns to be the keeper of the die. Any player wishing to have a shot pays the keeper one marble. He then shoots at the target from a predetermined distance. He must pay one marble for each shot he makes. If a player knocks the die off the marble with his shot, he receives from the keeper the number of marbles corresponding to the number shown uppermost on the die.

DOBBLERS

A game for any small number of players. Each player contributes one or more marbles to a straight line of marbles spaced so that there is room for two marbles to pass through the gaps. Each player then shoots in turn and may keep any marbles he hits. The player's Taw remains where it lies at the end of his turn and subsequent turns are played from where the Taw lies. A player whose Taw is hit by another Taw must add one marble to the line.

EGGS IN THE BUSH

This is a guessing game which requires no skill but is nevertheless entertaining. A player picks up a number of marbles with one hand and asks the other players to guess a number. Those guessing correctly are paid that number of marbles by the questioner. Those guessing incorrectly must pay the questioner the difference between the number guessed and the number actually held. Players take turns to be the questioner.

HANDERS (OR TIP-SHEARS)

A game of chance for several players which requires little skill. A hole 8cm (3in) wide is made about 30cm (1ft) from a wall. Each player throws a marble at the hole, from a predetermined spot, to decide the order of play. The person whose marble is closest to the hole starts, the second closest goes second, etc. Each player then contributes two marbles to the first player who throws them all at the hole. Any marbles that go in the hole are pocketed by the thrower. This does not apply to those that have rebounded off the wall, which remain in play. Those remaining are handed to the second player who makes his throw, and so play continues. When the marbles are exhausted a new contribution is made by all and the second player in the first round starts the second round.

HUNDREDS

A game for two players. A small circle is drawn or a small hole made at a suitable distance from the shooting spot. Both players shoot a marble towards the circle. If both or neither marble stops within the circle both players shoot again. If, however, only one player's marble stops within the circle, that player scores 10 points each time his marble stops in the circle on subsequent throws. This continues until he has scored 100 or until he misses. The first player to reach 100 points is the winner and the loser hands over a predetermined number of marbles.

INCREASE POUND

A game for several players. Two circles are drawn; one circle 20cm (8in) in diameter known as the pound and around it another of 3.5m (11ft) diameter called the 'bar'. Each player puts one or more marbles into the pound. The first player shoots a Taw from any point of the bar, at the marbles in the pound. Any marbles he knocks out of the pound become his property. If he fails to capture even one marble his Taw remains where it stops, if that is within the bar and outside the pound. If it stops within the pound it must be lifted and a marble paid to the pound.

Subsequent players may shoot at the pound or at an opponent's Taw. If a Taw is struck by another Taw, the owner of the struck Taw must give any marbles he has captured so far in the game to the owner of the Taw that struck his Taw.

LAG OUT

An order of play is decided by any number of players. Each player in turn throws a marble at a wall so as to make it rebound. The marbles are left where they fall until one player's marble rebounds and lands on another. That player then claims all the marbles on the floor and play is restarted.

LONG TAW

For two players. Each player contributes a marble and these are placed approximately 2m (6ft) apart. The players withdraw a further 2m (6ft) and the first player shoots his Taw at the first marble. If he hits it he pockets it and shoots at the second marble. If he hits that, he wins the round and the game starts again. If he fails to win the round outright the opponent shoots at the marbles and at the Taw. If the marbles are hit the result is as described for the first player. If he hits the Taw he captures whatever is on the ground.

A guessing game similar to Eggs in the Bush except that one has to guess whether it is an odd or even number of marbles in the hand of the questioner. Those who guess correctly receive a marble; those who are incorrect give one to the questioner. Each player takes it in turn to ask the question.

ONE STEP

This game is played like Dobblers except that a player takes one step and throws his Taw from a standing position when making his first shot. Subsequent throws are also made from the standing position but without making a step. A successful throw entitles the player to another throw from the spot where the Taw lies.

PICKING PLUMS

For a small number of players. A straight line is drawn on the ground and each player contributes one or more marbles, which are placed in a row on the line about 2 marbles' width apart. A parallel line is then drawn about 2m (6ft) away. Players stand behind this second line and take it in turns to shoot at the line of marbles (these marbles are the 'plums' of the game's title). A shot which knocks a plum out of the line entitles the player to the plum, but not to a second shot. Play continues until all plums are picked.

'Picking Plums' is illustrated on the following page.

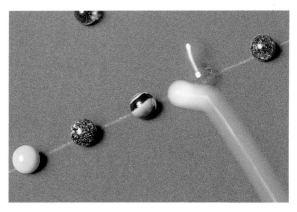

● *'Picking Plums' — a good test of shooting skill.*

PYRAMID

As in Archboard and Die Shot, someone has to be the keeper of the pyramid. This person draws a circle approximately 30cms (1ft) in diameter and places one marble on top of three to form a pyramid in the centre of the ring. The keeper then charges the players a marble for each shot at the pyramid. Any marbles knocked out of the ring become the property of the shooter and the pyramid has to be rebuilt by the keeper using his own marbles.

SPANNERS

A simple capturing game for two players. The first sends forth a marble. The second shoots to hit it and capture it. However, if his marble stops within a span of the opponent's marble he still takes it. A span is the distance between the spread thumb and forefinger of the biggest hand available. If he is unsuccessful, play passes to his opponent, who in turn tries to capture his marble.

RING TAW

This is one of the best known and most popular of all marble games for a group of players. As with Increase Pound, two circles are drawn on the ground. The inner circle should be about 30cm (1ft) in diameter, the outer should be about 2m (7ft) diameter. Each player puts an agreed number of marbles into the inner ring. The order of play is decided and the players take turns to shoot their Taws, from any point on the outer ring, at the marbles in the centre.

Any marbles knocked out of the centre ring are pocketed by the shooter and he is entitled to shoot again from the spot where his Taw lies. When a shot is unsuccessful play passes to the next player who may then shoot at the marbles in the centre or at any of the Taws. If he strikes a Taw, its owner pays him one marble and he takes another shot. He may not strike the same opponent's Taw twice in succession. The game continues until the ring is cleared.

OTHER GAMES

Another way of playing marbles is to create indoor miniature games from those usually played outside. The most obvious of these is marble bowls. However, croquet, golf and snooker can all be played with marbles on a carpet. With some cardboard, a pair of scissors and ingenuity, the necessary equipment can soon be made.

CHAPTER 5
MARBLE CHAMPIONSHIPS

The two best known Marble Championships in the world are the American Championship which takes place at Wildwood in New Jersey and the British Marble Championships which take place on Good Friday each year at the Greyhound Pub at Tinsley Green in Sussex. The main difference between the two championships is that, whereas the Wildwood championships are most definitely for children, the British Championships are for adults. Both are taken most seriously.

● **Sam Spooner** *at the British Marble Championships 1937.*

MEN'S BRITISH MARBLES CHAMPIONSHIP RULES
──────── T E A M   C H A M P I O N S H I P ────────

RING to be 6 feet in diameter made of concrete raised approximately 2 inches from ground.

THAT a Team consists of six players.

THAT each game is played between two teams.

THAT the winning team of each game is the team securing the most marbles. The winning team then passes into the next round and so on until the finals are reached.

The ***GAMES*** are commenced by the two Captains who hold Tolleys to their noses and drop them from there endeavouring to make them land on the outer circle. The Captain who gets on the ring or the nearest thereto shoots first followed by his opponent and so on in turn.

NOTE (Competitors must stand upright when dropping Tolley). The number of Marbles placed in the ring for each game is 49.

The Competitor shoots Tolleys and endeavours to knock marbles from the ring. If he succeeds and his Tolley remains in the ring he shoots again. If, however, a Competitor shoots and does not succeed in knocking Marbles from the ring, but his Tolley remains in the ring, he stays there until his turn comes round again. He then shoots from inside the ring, knuckles down on the sand. Rough sand to be used liberally on the pitch.

Size of Tolley to be $3/4$ inch in diameter and not exceed. No bottle tops.

Standard $1/2$ in diameter clay marbles must go in the ring.

TEAM OF SIX to pay two shillings and sixpence per head to cover printing, prizes, etc.

COMMITTEE to consist of Captains of Teams.

A set of rules from 1940s briefly sums up the rules and the game played at the British Championships. The game played is like Ring Taw (already described).

──────── OTHER USES OF MARBLES ────────

In a clear glass vase, marbles conceal and support flower stems. They can be used to hide the soil surface around a pot-plant, helping to keep in moisture. They look attractive at the bottom of a fish tank and provide a safe place for the fish to lay their eggs. These are only a few of many such decorative and practical uses.